Early Bird Gets The E

CW00409550

By Andrew K. Courey

Contact me if you have any questions or would like to tell me something about the book at andrewcourey34 goldenmamba@gmail.com. I will try to respond as soon as possible.

Forward

I am very passionate about cryptocurrencies and have read lots of books, articles, and blogs on the topic, in addition to watching many YouTube videos. They were all helpful, but I did not think anything really captured all the important points in plain language in one place with useful examples and analogies.

I wrote this book because a lot of people I know kept asking me the same questions about Bitcoin:
- What is Bitcoin?
- How does it work?
- Should I care about it?
- Am I too late to invest?
- What is Ethereum? How is it different than Bitcoin?
- Is this just a fad or is this a huge deal that will change the world?

This is my attempt to provide that one place to start – a true introduction to Bitcoin. To summarize the answers to a few of these questions:
- Yes, you should care.
- No, you are not too late.
- Yes, this a huge deal that *could* change the world, though it is still too early to know how huge.

Read on and enjoy!

Andrew K. Courey

Table of Contents

Introduction To Bitcoin

Today we will be learning about an online currency created by Satoshi Nakamoto, and by the end, you will become a master of Bitcoin. Here are the basics of Bitcoin.

Bitcoin is a kind of online money that you can use to buy things. Just like the U.S. dollar, you can buy it, sell it, and exchange it for stuff. Unlike the U.S. dollar (or other currencies like the Euro or Canadian dollar), it is not issued by a government, but exists outside of governments as a cryptocurrency. Cryptocurrencies are digital, not physical, meaning they are not coins, bills, or gold. The word crypto is how cryptocurrency is protected (we will cover this topic later in the book), and currency means money. When you put those words together, it means secure money. That is exactly what it is: secure digital money.

OK, so why would anyone want a cryptocurrency instead of a normal currency? The problem is that governments can print a lot of their currency whenever they want, so you cannot trust now much currency is out there. This matters because all types of currency are worth less the more of it that exists. This is called inflation. With Bitcoin, there is no inflation.

The great thing about Bitcoin is that there is a maximum amount of Bitcoin that will ever be created: 21 million. Once 21 million coins are mined, no more will be created ever. As of the writing of this book, 79% (around 16 million) of all Bitcoins have already been mined. People estimate that by 2024 all the Bitcoin will have been mined for good. Therefore, if you own Bitcoin you can be comfortable that a government will not print more of it and lower its value.

I just used a crazy word that normally does not get used with currencies: mining. Not the type of mining where you dig for gold in the ground, but quite similar. The Bitcoin creators designed a very clever system to combine the processes for creating Bitcoin with the process for verifying Bitcoin transactions. Sounds complicated, but do not worry - here is a brief explanation of how it works.

There is a public document that tracks all of the Bitcoin transactions ever in the history of Bitcoin - this is called a blockchain. Think of it as a public Google Docs file that everyone has access to. This is very powerful, because you cannot fake a transaction that everybody using Bitcoin can see.

So how does the system make sure everyone has the same copy of this blockchain and cannot change or edit it? The answer is Bitcoin miners, who use their computing power to continuously verify the latest block. A block is a group of all the transactions that have happened in ten minutes. By verifying these blocks, the miners are protecting against any fake transactions.

Why would anyone bother to use his or her computing power (which costs money) to do this? The answer is that by doing so they have a chance of earning more Bitcoin as a reward. Every ten minutes one block containing 12.5 Bitcoins is mined, and those Bitcoins are given to the lucky miner. 12.5 does not seem like a lot at first, but that could be worth upwards of $140,000.

When I say lucky, I mean that there is a lot of chance involved. A random 64-digit number is generated, and the computers have to guess that number while verifying transactions. Whoever guesses it first wins the block. As crazy as it sounds, this process keeps Bitcoin safe so that when you buy and sell Bitcoin, your balance is changed and continuously verified.

To hack the Bitcoin network, you would need billions of dollars in computing power, which would not be worth it. Bitcoin is stored in a wallet just like real money. The wallet is on your computer so no one can hack it, unlike other riskier ways of storing money. Bitcoin is safer than money because with physical money someone could pickpocket you or you could lose it. With Bitcoin, the only way to lose it is to lose your computer or your private key. Private keys are simply passwords that you need to make transactions.

One of the best things about Bitcoin is the fact that banks are not involved in Bitcoin. Normally you would give money to the bank and they would give it to the person you were trying to send money to, but with

Bitcoin it is different. The money you send goes directly to their Bitcoin wallet. This eliminates the middleman and makes sending and receiving money much simpler. To buy and sell Bitcoin, there is usually a fee of approximately 3%, although lower fee alternatives are being developed.

Just to be clear, Bitcoin is not stable - the price can change drastically in an hour. The U.S. dollar's value might change by only two or three percent per year, while Bitcoin might change two or three percent in a day. In some ways, it is a currency, but in others, it is an investment. If you had bought $1,000 in Bitcoin last year, it would be worth almost $20,000 now. It can also go down a lot and you could lose everything, perhaps making it similar to gambling. Bitcoin's volatility is responsible for many people getting rich and many people losing lots of money.

There are three ways to mine: on your own, in a pool, or cloud mine. If you mine on your own, you either get 12.5 Bitcoins (highly unlikely) or nothing, and you wasted electricity (more likely). Pools are basically groups of miners that get together to have higher odds of winning the block collectively, with an agreement to distribute the money proportionately afterwards. Their belief is that the more miners guessing the number, the better chances that someone in the group gets it right. With pools, you will consistently make money every day, but in small amounts. The better your computer/miner contributing to the pool is, the more money you will get. Lastly, cloud mining is the same as pool mining but instead of using your own miner you buy computer power. The cloud mining service keeps the computers in their warehouse. This is an option for mining if you do not have a lot of space.

You just learned the basics of Bitcoin. As you read on, we will explore these topics in great detail. The key things to remember are that Bitcoin is not physical, it is created through mining, and that it can be used just like real currency to buy stuff. Good luck on your journey of mastering Bitcoin!

History of Bitcoin

Let's talk about the creator of Bitcoin: Satoshi Nakamoto. Some people believe he was just a man named Satoshi Nakamoto, but others believe that Satoshi Nakamoto is not his real name and that he is somebody else. All we know for sure is that someone going by the name of Satoshi Nakamoto created Bitcoin. It is an unsolved mystery.

They have found a 70-year old man named Satoshi Nakamoto at birth, but he claims he has nothing to do with Bitcoin. There is a good chance that he is just a normal person, but maybe he really is the creator. The reason that name is associated with Bitcoin is that Bitcoin had a mailing list when it started, and Satoshi Nakamoto was the name on it. Hal Finney was the co-founder (and is not anonymous) - he says he does not know who Satoshi Nakamoto really is, and has never met him. A man from Australia named Craig Wright claimed he was the creator, but after being investigated, he admitted he was not.

Why is he remaining anonymous? I suspect the answer is that he is worried that he could get in serious legal trouble. Because the government cannot do anything about Bitcoin without his identity, remaining anonymous guarantees him to be safe.

Let's discuss the main candidates to be Satoshi Nakamoto: Nick Szabo, Dorian Nakamoto (the man born with the name Satoshi Nakamoto), and Elon Musk. All three of them have denied that they created Bitcoin, so we still have no idea. Two things can be certain about Satoshi Nakamoto: he knows 80,000 words (has used them on his posts), and that he is a super genius.

Now that you have a good understanding who created Bitcoin, let's talk about the history of Bitcoin.

In 2007, the idea for Bitcoin started when Satoshi Nakamoto started developing Bitcoin. On January 1, 2009, the first block was mined, and this block became known as the Genesis Block. Every subsequent block is based off of the Genesis Block. Eight days after the first block was mined, Bitcoin version 0.1 was released. Three days later, when block 170 was mined, a monumental moment in Bitcoin history occurred when the first Bitcoin transaction was made, from Satoshi Nakamoto to co-founder Hal Finney.

Every currency has an exchange rate like dollars to euros, and the same goes for Bitcoin. The original exchange rate set by New Liberty Standard was $1 = 1,309.03 Bitcoins. $1 worth of Bitcoin then would be worth over $20 million dollars now. Right now $1 will get you approximately 0.000067 Bitcoins instead of 1,309.03.

On February 6, 2010, Bitcoin was first available on an exchange. The first and dumbest real world transaction occurred when a programmer from Florida paid 10,000

Bitcoins for two pizzas. Little did he know that he paid $150 million dollars total, or $75 million dollars for each pizza! The day this happened, May 22, 2010, is forever known as Bitcoin Pizza Day.

On July 12, 2010, Bitcoin's price raised from $0.008 per Bitcoin to $0.08, which is a 1,000% increase, more than most investments make in 20 years. Five days later, Bitcoin joined a major exchange called MtGox and took the first steps into becoming what we know today as Bitcoin. Just under a month later, tragedy struck when Bitcoin was hacked, resulting in 184 billion Bitcoins being generated. This problem was later fixed, and the cap on Bitcoins ever in circulation was set back to 21 million. By November 6, 2010, the price was at $0.50 per Bitcoin, which is more than a 600% increase. By then the price was going up so much that more people started buying Bitcoin. The true highlight of 2010 was when the first mobile (on a phone) transaction occurred. Ever since December 8, 2010, mobile crypto-transactions have made cryptocurrency very popular.

In early 2011, an online store started selling illegal things online with Bitcoin because Bitcoin is untraceable. In the blockchain ledger (the online list with all the transactions - I will explain this in the next section as it is pretty complicated), the transaction history only uses your wallet address, not your real name. On February 9, 2011, the price of Bitcoin had now reached $1 dollar, helping people view it more as a legitimate currency. For example, soon after that someone sold their car for

Bitcoin because they trusted that Bitcoin as a currency worth having. On June 8, 2011, the price skyrocketed up to $32, causing many people who invested early to become millionaires.

Soon after, the phrase "Bitcoin bubble" started getting used a lot as the price collapsed in just a few days. The term bubble simply means the price is like a bubble - i.e. it expands a lot until it expands too much and...pop, Bitcoin just crashed! The reason I explained bubbles is because on June 12, 2011, after the massive price surge, the price dropped to less than $10 and people started calling Bitcoin unstable, or a bubble. In addition, on June 19, 2011, MtGox was hacked, impacting 60,000 users accounts, and subsequently shut down for seven days.

In June 2012, the most popular cryptocurrency exchange was founded in San Francisco, Coinbase. I use Coinbase myself because it is very simple to buy and sell because Coinbase does all the complicated stuff for you. Other people thought this too, so it changed Bitcoin forever, because it made buying Bitcoin as easy as ever. In November of that year, a valuable private company, Wordpress, started accepting Bitcoins as payment. Also, Bitcoin Central, a Bitcoin bank, got listed as an official European bank, making it even closer to a real currency. By the end of 2012, Bitcoin was an established currency and no longer just some fun new thing online. Real companies were trading Bitcoin for real products, because it had value.

In 2013, Bitcoin has a crazy year and a lot of unusual things happened, so let's get right into it. Early that year, Bitcoin's price was the same as the most valuable U.S. note, the $100 bill. With the price at $100, all the Bitcoins in circulation were worth a total of $1 billion dollars. Normally ATMs give you cash, but what if they gave you Bitcoin? That is what happened on May 2, 2013 in San Diego, when the first Bitcoin ATM was created. After the price went up for a few months, it fell from $139 to $110 in three hours in early October, when the FBI shut down a criminal black market (a place that sells illegal things) that was using Bitcoin to hide their identity. Later the price returned to $138 as people stopped worrying about what had happened.

On November 17, 2013, the price went all the way up to $503 the day before a Senate meeting about Bitcoin. The day after the hearing, Bitcoin skyrocketed to $1,242. Bitcoin was used for only basic payments up until November 22, when you could buy tickets to space with Bitcoin. On November 27, a multibillion-dollar company called Shopify added Bitcoin as one of their payment methods. This decision added potentially millions more Bitcoin users, due to Shopify's massive user base.

In February 2014, MtGox lost 744,000 Bitcoins, which is like 20 or 30 banks getting robbed at once, with everybody's money gone and no trace of the criminals.

Like the New York Stock Exchange where you can trade stocks, Coinbase made a place where you can exchange Bitcoin. From the start of 2016 to the end of 2017 Bitcoin has went from around $400 to currently around $11,000. And, as they would say, "the rest is history."

Congratulations on finishing the history of Bitcoin section - hopefully you learned a lot. My objective was to give you a better idea of the journey that Bitcoin took from its start in 2009 to where we are right now in 2018.

Fun Fact: If you invested $1 in Bitcoin at the very start, you would have approximately $20 million dollars now (WOW!). All this shows you that if you invest your money smartly and carefully, it will pay off in the future.

What Is Blockchain

To put blockchain into simple terms, it is just a file with every transaction ever made. But blockchain is much more complicated than that. In this section I will go into detail about how blockchain works, and will give you a better idea of why it is so secure, and much more.

Blockchain is what keeps Bitcoin and other cryptocurrencies so secure, because it keeps track of everybody's transactions. Miners are working to verify every transaction. Your balance is calculated based on your transactions listed on the blockchain, so you cannot spend the same Bitcoin twice. Once it is spent, it is gone. Normally when hosting a database, there is a giant computer somewhere, but with blockchain, it is stored on everybody's computers. Anyone with a computer can access blockchain and verify transactions, making it as public as possible. As I said earlier, blockchain is basically a Google Docs file shared with everyone that can only be edited by buying or selling Bitcoin. The only way someone can change it is by making a transaction.

If you are wondering why there have been so many hacks, it has nothing to do with blockchain - instead, it is actually websites that hold people's Bitcoin that are being hacked. Hackers figured out that you cannot hack the blockchain, but you can hack websites. If you are storing your Bitcoin on a computer or a USB drive, you will likely not be hacked - just do not lose your computer/USB drive!

Every ten minutes the blockchain adds up all the transactions and creates a block that people can then verify. Why would people verify transactions? As I mentioned in the introduction, they do so because they have a chance of winning newly issued Bitcoins. This motivates many people to mine Bitcoin, which is what keeps the network going. To create a fake transaction, you would need more than half of the power of the network, which would cost billions of dollars. The more users verifying transactions on the blockchain, the more secure it becomes every day. Many of the other cryptocurrencies use blockchain because it is so secure.

In the future, blockchain might be used for other things on the internet, like online banking or secure data storage. The blockchain file with all the transactions is called a ledger. For example, if I am trying to send one Bitcoin to someone, I tell the network to send one Bitcoin to the person's address, then the network will add one to their balance and subtract one from my balance. This process is all automated - all the user has to do is enter the amount of Bitcoin they want to spend.

An issue with the blockchain is that if something goes wrong, you cannot go to the government, and you cannot call customer support. This is because blockchain is owned by everybody, not one person or company you can get help from. On the ledger, your public key (your address) is displayed, not your real name or any information about you.

There are 1,461,501,637,330,902,918,203,684,832,716, 283,019,655,932,542,976 different possible wallet addresses, which means it is impossible to guess someone's address, and that the number of address will never run out. All transactions inside a block will be considered to be made at the same time. Everyone has a public and private key. Everyone has access to the public key, but the private key is the password you need to spend or exchange Bitcoins, so no one but the owner has access to it.

Blockchain is decentralized, unlike traditional currencies. For example, the U.S. government decides when to print money and how much money to print – this is a centralized model. Bitcoin, however, is decentralized, which means the no individual or organization has control of the money supply or generating more money. The U.S. government could start printing $1 million dollar bills tomorrow, and we would all have to go with it. The only way Bitcoin could create one million more Bitcoins is if everybody together started mining more Bitcoins. The power is held by everyone with decentralization, and held by a few institutions with centralization. Normally if I was trying to sell something, I would need a middleman like a bank, or eBay, but with blockchain you are sending or receiving directly to/from the other person. If you buy sports tickets online, you would need Seatgeek or StubHub, but if you bought them in person it would just be you and that other person. The great thing about blockchain is that all of this is done automatically without you doing a thing.

The software that does all of the transaction related stuff is called a smart contract. Let me give you an example: if I was betting $100 with someone on whether it was going to rain or snow, we would have three options to set this up. The first way would be to base it on trust, which would work if we were friends, but not if we were strangers. The second option would be to make a contract and both sign it. If someone broke the contract, it would cost more than $100 in legal expenses to fix it, which would also be bad. This leaves us with only one other option: we could both give that $100 to a third party, who would then check the weather and give the money to the winner. That is what smart contracts are - they eliminate the ability to scam somebody because the power is in the smart contract's hands. Because smart contracts are computer code, they cannot steal, because they have not ever been programmed to steal. The way a smart contract "thinks" is that it scans for a trigger, and then it executes the code it was told to do after the triggering event. A triggering event can be anything from someone did not pay on time, or if the digital assets I bought had not arrived. The code it executes is meant to fix the problem, such as giving someone a refund. In real life, you could lose your contract, but with Bitcoin the contract is saved on a shared and encrypted (secured) ledger.

Smart contracts have an issue in common with normal contracts, which is that if you write the wrong thing, it will still be executed. One final thing on smart contracts is that you can write your own with Ethereum. Go to www.Ethereum.org and download the app, which will take a few minutes. You cannot get started just yet, because you first need to learn the basics of solidity (the Etherum programming language) which you can learn at https://solidity.readthedocs.io/en/develop/introduction-to-smart-contracts.html, or at https://Ethereumbuilders.gitbooks.io/guide/content/en/solidity_tutorials.html. Online courses are also available.

Let's talk about the future of blockchain and how it will have a significant impact on money as it becomes more popular. Although the ways banks keep track of balances is very secure, it is nothing compared to blockchain. Blockchain will allow banks to pay less transaction costs but drastically improve the speeds at which the transactions are made. For blockchain to be implemented into banks, you would need every bank to use it. If only a few banks use it, blockchain will not work well. If, on the other hand, all the banks use blockchain, the network will be highly secure and take banking security to another level.

Will this get rid of normal currency? Maybe, but highly unlikely. One thing that will prevent Bitcoin (or other cryptocurrencies) from replacing cash is that Bitcoin is unstable. The U.S. dollar's value generally stays the same each year relative to other currencies, while

Bitcoin can change in value significantly every day. People might choose to use cash over Bitcoin because of its stability. To sum it all up, I think both will exist in the future and both will be used, but Bitcoin might someday start to be used as much as cash.

Congratulations, you finished the What Is Blockchain chapter and now know a lot about blockchain. You learned how it works, why it is secure, how smart contracts work, and what the future of blockchain could look like.

Fun Fact: People say that "imitation is the sincerest form of flattery." The creator of Bitcoin must be really flattered, because since the creation of Bitcoin over 1,379 cryptocurrencies have been created, which is more than 7 times the amount of other physical currencies in the world.

Bitcoin Wallets

In this chapter, we are going to discuss what a Bitcoin wallet is, different types of wallets, how to get started, and the security of Bitcoin wallets. Think of a Bitcoin wallet as a wallet that can store Bitcoin, because it is just that.

Bitcoin wallets are pieces of software that you can store Bitcoins in and send Bitcoins from. The idea of a Bitcoin wallet is very similar to a cash wallet, but when you break it down, they are very different. Bitcoin wallets are stored on your computer, just like you might keep your cash wallet in a box. The thing is that if you stole a cash wallet you could spend and receive all the money. If you stole a Bitcoin wallet, you could only receive Bitcoin, because it is protected by something called a private key. The private key is like the password and the public key is like the username. Anyone can access the public key, but only the owner of the wallet knows the private key. Imagine there is a mailbox - the mailman can drive the mail to any mailbox, but only the person with the key can access the mail.

The way the private key is generated is by putting the public key through an algorithm, called hashing. It is so complicated it would take more than a lifetime to figure the algorithm out. Private keys are unguessable because they are 51 digits - you have a better chance to win the lottery then to guess someone's private key. The private key is stored in the wallet, so if you lose your private key, you lose all your Bitcoin, because your wallet address and its balances are stored on the blockchain.

If someone obtained your private key, the person could change your public key. The new public key will still have all your Bitcoin and the same private key. These new keys are all linked to your seed, which is a phrase made up of 10-20 random words, which is also the only way to recover your wallet. I recommend that you write the phrase on a piece of paper and store it in a safe place.

There are many different ways to store your Bitcoin - we are going to go over all of them   in a few pages, but first I need to explain a couple of things. All of these different ways of storing Bitcoin are effective, but choosing one is all about what you need. I am going to compare the five different types and help you make a decision. The five types are offline, online, USB, paper, and mobile.

The safest option of all five is the offline wallet, because no one can access it through the internet. On the internet, someone could steal your private key, but being offline guarantees no one has access to your wallet. A wallet can be either cold or hot - a cold wallet is online, a hot wallet is offline. When you have an online wallet, your Bitcoins are being stored in the cloud, not on your computer.

Places like Coinbase have a wallet that contains your Bitcoins, but it is not as secure because Coinbase could get hacked. For example, if your account password get stolen, the hackers will have access to your Bitcoins, guessing a password is quintillions (one billion billion) of times easier than guessing a private key. The companies do have security to protect against hacks, but it is not guaranteed that if you store your Bitcoin online, it will not get stolen.

Mobile wallets are in between offline and online in terms of security because it is offline, but someone could get your Bitcoins if you lost your phone, which is more likely than losing your computer. It is safer than online but riskier than offline because, again, you could lose your phone. With mobile cryptobanks getting more popular, storing Bitcoin on your phone is very similar to something like Apple Pay.

Even though Bitcoin is not physical, you can still have a paper wallet, just like rewards points are not physical, but you can still pay with a rewards card. The way you can do this is by printing your Bitcoin address or QR code onto a piece of paper and then storing it along with the private key in a safe place. When you want to spend your Bitcoin, just take out the wallet, scan the QR code, and enter in your private key. This method is safe if you do it right. If you put it somewhere in a random drawer, it is not secure, but if you keep it in a safe or in a locked box, it is as secure as storing gold in a vault. I recommend you keep small amounts of money on it. To put it simply, paper wallets are like Bitcoin credit cards, and you do not want to lose your credit card.

The final way to store Bitcoin is with a USB drive, which is very similar to storing your wallet on your computer. In case you do not know what a USB drive is, it is basically a tiny portable hard drive that you can store files on. Because USBs are not connected to the internet, they are very safe. However, there are two issues: USBs are small and easy to lose, and USBs can get destroyed. USBs are usually about 1-2 inches, which means they are easy to lose. People lose their house keys every day, so it is very possible that you could lose your USB drive. The second issue is that because they are so small, if it falls it might break and you could lose all your data, including your Bitcoin. To sum this all up, the best option is the option used originally in 2009, storing your wallet on your computer offline. There is no risk and as long as no one steals your computer there is no way to get hacked.

Note: some wallets might give you a string of 12 random words. This is the only way to recover your account if you get locked out for any reason. This is similar to your private key.

Now that you know how wallets work, let's learn about how to get started. I will teach you how to get started with all five types of wallets.

First we have the offline wallet, there are many to choose from. I suggest that you consider the wallet from Bitcoin.org. First click resources, and then click Bitcoin Core. Bitcoin Core is the official wallet coming directly from the Bitcoin creators, which makes it secure. Once you are on Bitcoin core, scroll down and click "Get Started With Bitcoin." Click desktop, and then choose your operating system (if you do not know, click the Apple or Windows on the high left corner of your screen). Lastly, click Bitcoin Core and click install (it will take a few minutes). Note: if you do not have a lot of space on your computer this might not be the option for you. Because this wallet contains the blockchain ledger, it is 145 gigabytes (GB). If your computer has less than 256 GB, go with a different option. If you want, you could buy a one terabyte external hard drive from Western Digital. Make sure to write down your private key in notes for when you need it.

For the next option, online, I suggest you consider Coinbase, which is the most widely used online Bitcoin exchange. First go to Coinbase.com, and click sign up. Once you enter all your information, you will have an account, but cannot do anything with it. To be able to buy Bitcoin, you need a payment method - go to settings, and click add a payment method. To buy and sell, all you have to do is click buy/sell and add payment methods, and Coinbase does the rest.

Now for USBs - it is very similar to computers but with one extra step. Follow the steps from the Bitcoin Core Wallet, and then plug a USB into your computer, then go the finder app (or the Windows equivalent), and search for Bitcoin Core. Drag the file that says Bitcoin Core to under devices where it says flash drive, and enter. You can access that file by plugging the USB into any computer and clicking on it.

The paper wallet is the simplest because all you have to do is print something. First, go to "my address" (on your Bitcore wallet), copy the address, paste it in notes, then print. Then go to notes and print your private key the same way. Put the one with the private key locked in a box or hidden so it will not get lost or stolen. Then take the paper with the public address, fold it, and put it in your wallet. You can receive with the one in your wallet but you cannot spend any Bitcoin.

Finally, mobile Bitcoin wallets are relatively easy to set up. They all work just about the same, but if I had to choose, I would choose the wallet by Bitcoin.com. First, install the app, and then create an account. The fees to buy from Bitcoin.com are way too high, so If you really want a mobile wallet, follow these steps. Make an account at www.gdax.com, and then when you buy Bitcoin, send it to your mobile Bitcoin address. Do not do this every day because the fees will add up and you will lose money. If you are paying 1% every day, make one big deposit.

Congratulations on finishing the Bitcoin wallets chapter - you learned what it is, how it works, the different types, and now know how to create your own wallet.

Fun Fact: You are more likely to win the lottery and have your ticket struck by lightning in the same day than to correctly guess someone's private key.

Bitcoin Mining

What is mining? How does it work? Why mine? How much money can I make? All of these questions will be answered in the next chapter of this book. Mining is how Bitcoins are created, but there is a lot more to Bitcoin mining than that.

What is mining? Normally the way currency is put into circulation is the government prints more money. Bitcoin is different. A simple but huge difference is that the government can print as much currency as they want, but there can only be 21 million Bitcoins, ever. In order to keep the blockchain's transaction secure, the transactions need to be verified - that is where miners come in. The job of miners is to verify transactions to keep the network going, and in exchange the network rewards them with newly generated Bitcoin. When someone mines the block (we will talk about that in the next section), they get 12.5 Bitcoins. The odds of winning a block are very low, so people created things called pools. Pools are a group of miners that have good odds of winning the block because they have so much combined computing power. Each person in the pool does not get 12.5 Bitcoins. Instead, they are divided among the members based on how they contributed.

Mining solo (on your own) is not a good option unless you have millions of dollars to invest in equipment. Mining in a pool is much smarter in my opinion. Because you are being paid a set amount of Bitcoins each day, if

Bitcoin's price goes down you would make less, but if it goes up you would make more. To mine you need a powerful computer specially built for Bitcoin mining. Or you could do cloud mining which is basically mining Bitcoin using someone else's facility. The way it works is you rent a miner using their space, and get a commission on the money that miner makes. Lastly, you can mine other cryptocurrencies, since mining is not specific to Bitcoin but originated from Bitcoin. All of the top cryptocurrencies are mineable, which is why they are secure.

How does Bitcoin mining work? Let me take you through the mining process, then I will explain each part in detail. First, the miners verify if the transactions are valid with a complicated software they run on their computers. Second, all of these transactions are put into a block that can then be mined. Third, the current block and the past block are hashed to create a 64 hexadecimal number. A hexadecimal number is a number with 16 possibilities. Normal numbers have ten possibilities, but hexadecimal numbers have the numbers 0 through 9 and A,B,C,D,E,F as possibilities. The number of different possible hash numbers is incredibly huge. The miners guess this number with their computers until they guess it right and win the block. The more powerful miners have the best odds of guessing the block. Think about it this way: you are playing a game with two other friends, and one friend is thinking of a number from 1 to 100. You can guess as many times as you want at two guesses per second, and your friend can only make one guess per second. If you both guess for 10 seconds, you would have guessed 20 numbers, giving you 20% chance of guessing it right, and your friend would have guessed 10 times, giving him a 10% chance of getting it right. Both of you could have guessed it right, but you have better odds because you could guess more times per second. Mining products all have something called a hash rate. A computer with a 10th/second hash rate is twice as likely to win a block then a computer with a 5th/second hash rate.

Why mine Bitcoin? Over the years that question has got harder to answer because the difficulty increases. When I say the difficulty increases, I mean that it gets harder and harder each year because more people are using the network. At the very start of Bitcoin, you could have mined 10 blocks a day, because only 20-30 people were mining. Now that millions of people are mining, it is much less likely you successfully mine a block.

With that said, Bitcoin mining can be a good investment, but there are a few factors deciding that. The first factor is the current price of Bitcoin, which affects the return on your investment. After you invest a fixed amount in mining, the returns will determined by the price of Bitcoin. The second factor is mining technology. Even if your investment is working well in the short term, other miners may develop more efficient advanced mining technology that improves their hash rate. As a result, there is also a big risk to Bitcoin mining: like I said, you could buy thousands of dollars in equipment and you get a lot of Bitcoin initially, and then see your returns go down over time. If you look into buying a miner, they will give you an estimated daily return, but this is only the current number. Unfortunately, the money you will make each day will vary. Always remember: there are never any guarantees, all you can do is find the most likely way to make money.

Can I make money mining? The short answer is yes, but there is much more to it. It largely depends on if you are mining solo, in a pool, or cloud mining. Let's talk about solo mining first. The solo mining approach is "go big or go home." In other words, you could make a lot or absolutely nothing. It is just like the lottery, because you pay a few dollars in electricity costs for a chance at a lot of money. No matter how powerful your miner is, you will never make more than 12.5 Bitcoins in a block. To be successful with solo mining the only option is to invest millions of dollars to create a huge Bitcoin mining rig. Just to make it clear, I would suggest that you do not solo mine.

Now let's talk about one of the other ways you can make money with Bitcoin mining: pool mining. I do not like this option because it is too complicated to evaluate and it usually involves lots of fees that lower your return. The costs of electricity and all the other costs involved in pool mining is so complicated, it is not worth figuring out.

Instead, let's talk about cloud mining, which is in my opinion the best way to mine. Cloud mining is pool mining without storing equipment in your house and the associated complicated costs. As with all mining, the specific return depends on which cloud mining vendor you invest with, as well as the price of Bitcoin. In addition, if the Bitcoin yield per block changes (likely for the worst, in which each block would yield fewer Bitcoins), the mining returns would be impacted.

Congratulations on finishing this chapter on mining. Let's sum up all that we talked about in this section. We learned that mining is how Bitcoins are created. We learned that mining is when computers verify transactions and guess numbers to win blocks. We learned that cloud mining is the most profitable way to mine. Most importantly, we learned that nothing is a guarantee, so all you can do is find the option with the best odds of helping you succeed.

Fun Fact: Currently the power consumption of Bitcoin mining is estimated to be more than that of 159 countries, and if all the Bitcoin miners formed a country, it would likely be number 61 on the list of countries using the most power.

Potential Cloud Mining Services

https://hashflare.io/r/9990E5F4
https://pool.Bitcoin.com/index_en.html

Bitcoin Hacks

In this chapter, we are going to learn about Bitcoin hacks and what causes them. The Bitcoin network is secure, but hackers do not care and have found ways to steal Bitcoin.

Bitcoin is the most secure thing in the world because of cryptography, but there are a few well-known ways to "hack" it.

The first way to hack is to create fake transactions, but the miners would stop that. But what if you controlled all the miners? If you put billions of dollars into building a mining rig that is more than 50% of all the mining power, you could verify fake transactions. The reason this has not happened is because all the people with the billions of dollars needed to do this are publicly known, and they would go to prison. What if a government decided to do this? They could not get in trouble with the government, because they are in charge and there is not an "international" police force. It would also probably spark an international crisis. In the future, if the price of Bitcoin continues to go up, governments might try to do this, though the odds are very low. As the amount of mining power increases, 50% of the total mining power will likely cost many billions of dollars.

The second way of hacking Bitcoin would be to figure out someone's private key. Later in this chapter we will talk about other kinds of hacks, but I am just explaining the basics in this section. To figure out someone's private key, you could do one of two things. First, you could hack into the database of private keys and log into someone's account. Second, you could trick someone into entering that information.

The last and best way to hack Bitcoin is to hack an online exchange. Online exchanges store all of your Bitcoins with your account data, which means that if someone stole your password, they could transfer all your Bitcoin to their account. An important thing to remember is to never try to hack Bitcoin because you could end up in jail.

The first Bitcoin hack occurred in June 2011, when $250 million dollars worth of Bitcoins were stolen from a man's computer. Back in 2011, mining Bitcoins with a normal laptop could get you thousands of Bitcoins. This was the simplest of the Bitcoin hacks, because all someone did was log into his computer. The second Bitcoin hack occurred two months later, when someone stored their Bitcoins on an online wallet service that scammed them. What they did was claim that the site was hacked, but all they did was shut it down to steal his Bitcoin.

In March 2012, the biggest hack since the start of Bitcoin happened when $645 million dollars worth of Bitcoin were stolen. They then promised to pay everybody back (it was only worth a few hundred thousand back then). They were hacked again in May of that year and had to shut down their website. Are you noticing a pattern here? Great, because I am noticing that the Bitcoin network is never the problem, it is always human error. In the summer of 2012, yet another hack occurred when Bitfloor was hacked. When something is encrypted, it is very hard to hack, but when they backed up the file with everyone's private keys, they did not encrypt it, so the hackers stole everyone's accounts. I could talk about every hack ever, but there are just too many, so we will only discuss the top three.

The biggest hack in history was of MtGox, where 750,000 Bitcoins were taken, which is almost $10 billion dollars at today's prices. There were no refunds made for anybody, which meant that if you invested your life savings in Bitcoin, is was all gone. MtGox had been a company with many issues for a long time. First of all, any person working at the company could change other people's files. The biggest issue with MtGox is that only one person could change the company's code, Mark Karpeles, the main owner. That meant that bugs took weeks to fix. Apparently, some employees thought that the source code was a complete mess. This situation remains the biggest Bitcoin hack in history.

Now that you learned about the MtGox hack, let's learn about the second biggest hack, the Bitfloor hack we talked about earlier. In this case, 24,000 Bitcoins were stolen, which is equal to over $250 million dollars, but this time all the customers got their money back. There is not much to say about this hack other than: bad security = easy to hack.

The last hack we are going to talk about is the Bitfinex hack, where 120,000 Bitcoins, or over $1.3 billion dollars, were taken. Normally a Bitcoin wallet has one key, but with Bitfinex their wallets were connected with a wallet called BitGo which had three private keys. Bitfinex only stored two of those keys, so BitGo had to co-sign every transaction. The hackers stole two keys from people's BitFinex accounts, which allowed them to get the third key from BitGo and transfer people's Bitcoins to their accounts.

This wraps up everything about hacks that have happened and how. Now I am going to explain what security will protect against this in the future.

What is the future of digital security? Every day passwords are stolen, and every few months millions of dollars are stolen. As you can imagine, many companies are working to improve digital security. What has kept companies like Coinbase from being hacked is the fact that they use something called two-factor authentication. What that means is that normally you would log in with one password, but with two-factor authentication, you have to log in two ways. First, you have to enter your normal password, then after that they send a code to your phone, that you also have to enter.

The reason this is secure is that it is easier to steal a password than a phone. With that said, people lose their phones every day, plus phones get stolen. This is a good security option, but the problem lies in the company, not the user. As this is very secure, people still get hacked every day. As better security methods are being developed, this will be less of a problem. Apple has improved this a lot with the combination of two-factor authentication and Apple's Touch ID. This adds a third, much harder, step for hackers, because they now need to steal the password, phone, and fingerprint. Touch ID is based on the fact that every human has a unique fingerprint, even identical twins. The only possible way to hack a fingerprint scan is to take a picture of someone's hand and scan it as a fingerprint. The huge issue with this is that it only works on iPhones, which leaves Android users stuck. Some Android phones are using their own version of Touch ID, which is useful but not all Android phones have it.

How are there still hacks? Because not all users of online Bitcoin exchanges use two-factor authentication, and not all exchanges use it either. Before the end of this chapter, I would like to explain one more thing: market manipulation is legal with Bitcoin. Market manipulation is when someone spreads fake news about a company by telling people or posting it on the internet. It is, however, illegal in the stock market, because it is cheating. Imagine you are the owner of a popular media company and you own a lot of Bitcoin, do you want it to go up or down? Up, of course, because you want to make money. So what if you posted a story about how China is about to buy $1 billion dollars of Bitcoin, the price would go up. Even if you completely made up that story, people would believe it and the price would go up. This could also be opposite as fake news could make Bitcoin go down. This is a big disadvantage of Bitcoin not being connected to the government. This is partly why Bitcoin is very unstable and risky. Let me leave you with a quote from me: "hackers versus security is a never ending war."

Congratulations on learning about Bitcoin hacks - you learned about some major hacks, how they happened, and the future of online security. Just remember: as the hackers get smarter, the security will get stronger, and as the security gets stronger, the hackers will up their game.

Fun Fact: The amount stolen in the MtGox hack was the same as robbing 2 million small banks, and the hackers did not even get caught.

Investing In Bitcoin

Before we go in depth about investing in Bitcoin, there are a few important things you should know. First, Bitcoin is not a normal kind of investment, it is in its own class. Bitcoin does not represent ownership of a company (like a stock), of land (like real estate), or of something tangible in the real world. Every other kind of investment represents one of those three things, but Bitcoin has value solely because of the supply and demand. That is the main reason why Bitcoin is more unstable than other types of investments.

This leads me to my second point: you could lose all your money. We all believe that if we have $100 today in cash that that money will still be worth $100 tomorrow. However, with Bitcoin you cannot be sure. If you invested all your money in Bitcoin, and then China banned Bitcoin, you could lose 99% of your money. There is much risk with Bitcoin, but with much risk comes much reward. In a single day Bitcoins price could go up by 10% or it could go down by that much. With the stock market, it usually takes a year for a company's stock price to change by that much. A good way to think about it is as volatile investing, as it might only take one or two weeks investing in Bitcoin to double your money or to cut it in half.

The last topic I would like to address before we go in depth is why you should consider investing in Bitcoin compared to other things. The short answer to that is that you could get rich fast, but the long answer is more complicated. If you invested $1,000 in stocks and made 10% per year, it would take a little more than 7 years to double your money, but if you made 10% a day, it would only take 7 days to double your money. A lot of people have $1,000 or more in the bank and they want more as soon as possible. $1,000 is not a huge amount of money to risk, and that $1,000 could have turned into $15,000 if you invested at the end of 2016.

We are going to cover four topics in this chapter: how to invest, why you should or should not, how much money you could make, and the truth about investing in cryptocurrency.

How to invest: First, let's look at what investing is and what is its purpose. Investing is a kind of system where you put something in and get something out - you can invest in all kinds of things from a lemonade stand to a $100 million dollar company. Like all things, there is a risk and a potential reward. Let me give you two examples. First, your friend wants to borrow $100 from you to sell cookies, because he needs that money to pay for the ingredients. Your friend promises to give you $120 at the end of the bake sale, which is a 20% gain. The second example is very different: this time you want to sell a special drink you made, but you do not have the ingredients to make it. You invest $100 of your own money to make the drinks and sell them for $120 total, which is a 20% profit. Both options make you $20, but which is better? Most people would say they are equal, but an investor would say the second one was better. That is because with the first option, you had no control over whether you made that 20% because your friend was running the business and just needed your money. This means there is a much higher risk of losing the $100 and much lower chance of making the 20%. With the second option, you have full control of what you do with the $100 and can improve the odds you make money. If you do this once with both options you might think the first one is better, but if you did this 100 times, you would make more money with the second option. This is a way of thinking that will help you become successful if you apply it to any investment. To apply this to Bitcoin, think about the chances of it going up and the chances of it going down. Next figure out what you think the odds of it going up are, and if they are above 50% buy it, and if they are below 50%, do not buy it.

Should I invest? The answer to that question depends on a few things that define a good Bitcoin investment. The first of those things is if you have the money to invest, only invest the money you can afford to lose. Although it is possible that you could get rich from Bitcoin, it is also possible that you lose all of it. A good way to find how much money you should invest is by taking the total amount of money used for things that are not essentials and divide that by 1.5. This will insure that if you lose all of it that you will not go bankrupt and you will not have any financial issues. If you are a kid trying to invest in Bitcoin, I recommend putting whatever you are comfortable with and save up money over time to invest once it builds up. If you make $10 every day for a year, you will have $3,650 to invest in Bitcoin.

The next factor that should help you decide if you want to invest in Bitcoin is why. There are three intentions people have when buying Bitcoin: to make money, to buy things with it, and to own Bitcoin because it is cool. If you are looking to own Bitcoin for the sake of it, just buy $10 and leave it at that. The first two options are a little more complicated. If you are investing to make money, Bitcoin is a great option and has made people money in the past. If you believe that Bitcoin's price will increase, buy Bitcoin, otherwise wait until you think it will go up. If making money is your intention, you should view as Bitcoin an investment, not a currency. If you want to use Bitcoin as a payment method, by buying it you are making an investment. Remember that if you do not have an idea of what you think the price will be, you could have $100 in Bitcoin saved up for new shoes and the next day you only have $90 and no longer can buy the shoes. If you are going to use Bitcoin for payment, make sure you know a lot about it. By the end of this book, you should be a Bitcoin expert, and will have the mental tools to decide if you want to invest.

How much money can you make? There are two things to know about how much money can you make: how much money other people have made, and what you would expect to make. First, let's talk about how much money people have made, which in total is a lot. If you had bought $1 worth of Bitcoins in 2009 you would have more than $15,000,000 now. However, this beyond insane value increase since 2009 only would have occurred if you had bought it at the very start. If you had bought $1 worth in 2010, you would have gained 75,000%, which would have turned your $1 into $750. To put that into perspective, at a normal 10% increase per year it would take just less than 70 years to make 750 times your money vs the 7 years it took Bitcoin to increase by that much. You probably get the idea - you could have made a lot if you had bought Bitcoin when it started. One last example: if you had bought it at the start of 2017, you would have made 15 times your money.

Now, let's discuss how much you can expect to make in the future. No one knows the answer to that question, but people have made good predictions. I think that the price of Bitcoin is like waves on the ocean. It goes up and down, some days more than others, but eventually sets at a stable point (price). The only thing that is almost guaranteed is that in 2024 the price will be much higher, assuming that it does not get banned in any countries. This is because in the year 2024 the last Bitcoin will be mined, and we know that when demand increases while supply stays flat, the price usually goes up. One thing to remember is that the price will either go up by a lot or down by a lot, with Bitcoin there is no stability. The rest is a mystery that will be uncovered in the next few years.

The truth about investing in cryptocurrency: Cryptocurrency is a very different investment (as opposed to stocks and real estate) that comes with great risk and great reward. If you invest in cryptocurrency you could make or lose money, just like any other investment. There are so many factors in deciding if you should invest. It is all a game of timing, if you buy it on the days its price is low and sell it on the days its price is high. The best way to become a cryptocurrency investor is to learn everything about it and keep up with the latest news. Good ways to learn about cryptocurrency are to read books, read articles, watch Youtube videos, and practice investing with $10. These sources will all teach you different skills that you can use in all types of investing. Another point I would like to bring up is that nothing about Bitcoin is a sure answer. Every price prediction could be wrong, every country could ban Bitcoin, or the price could go up to $1 million dollars and become the official U.S. currency (low odds).

Congratulations on finishing the investing in Bitcoin chapter - let's recap what we have learned. You learned how to invest and if you should or should not. You learned how investing works, how to think about risk and reward, and that the balance between risk and reward is what determines if you should buy something. We talked about how much money you could make and what type of investment Bitcoin is. Let me leave you on one thing before the fun fact: by mastering Bitcoin investing, you are mastering all types of investing.

Fun Fact: If you bought 1309.03 Bitcoins instead of buying a $1 drink in 2009 you could buy 19 million of that $1 drink in 2018.

Bitcoin Crash

In this chapter, we are going to learn about Bitcoin crashing. What is a crash? What causes crashes? What would happen if it did crash? Those questions are the questions we are going to find answers to in this chapter. Also, we will figure out the chances that Bitcoin crashes at some point.

What is a crash? A crash is when an asset loses a lot of value. Let me give you a real world example of a crash. Imagine that everyone in your town was buying this new phone that costs $900 from a retail store. Then someone who thought the phone was too expensive bought it online for $500. The person then sold the phone for $850, which would make everyone's phones now worth 5.6% less, which is not a crash. A crash would occur if that person found the phone online for $100 and sold it for $200. The reason the second scenario was a crash and the first was not, is because the value went down significantly for the second option but not the first. Another way to think about it is as follows: imagine you are at the beach and the waves are normally 5 feet high, but then you see a 6-foot wave. The wave was not a tsunami because it was not that much bigger than the normal waves. The way to apply this to Bitcoin is simple: if the price goes down by 25% or more it is a crash, otherwise it is not.

Crashes can happen in different time spans: in a day, a week, a month, or even a year. Crashes that happen in a day are less likely than crashes that happen in a year, because something drastic would have to happen for something to crash in a day. The more common situation that happens is something goes down a lot in one day, and then goes down steadily the rest of the year. Crashes could happen to everything, from a type of drink to a $500 billion dollar company. One good thing to know about crashes is that they are rumored to happen via the internet. These media sources could be right or could be wrong, but you can always check for the latest price to see for yourself. When there is an article about Bitcoin possibly crashing, remember that no one knows how, when, or if Bitcoin will crash. Crashes are unpredictable just like Bitcoin going up is unpredictable. Be aware of fake news!

There are things you can do to make a good guess on if there will be a crash. Those things include reading articles about crashes and keeping up with the latest Bitcoin news. You can read articles by searching "Bitcoin Crash" or "Will Bitcoin crash?" and you can keep up with the news through Bitcoin newsletters and blogs.

What causes crashes? Crashes can be caused by anything, but some causes are more frequent than others. Let's take a look at three examples of what has caused crashes in the past, the stock market crash, Bitcoin crash, and Litecoin crash. There was a stock market crash in 2008 where almost every stock lost value, when banks could not pay large loans. That led to banks going bankrupt, and a lot of companies that had their money in banks lost some/all of it. That made the company's stock less valuable, and because this happened to many companies, the whole market crashed. What happened in 2008 is similar to what happened with MtGox, MtGox lost all their money and so did the people who stored their Bitcoins in MtGox.

To understand how Bitcoin could crash in the future, let's find out what happened in December 2017. On December 17, the price of Bitcoin was near $20,000, up from around $10,000 at the start of the month. The price of Bitcoin then went from $20,000 to $13,000, which is a 35% decrease in price. This crash was caused by a few different reasons; let's take a look at each. The main reason for the crash is transaction costs (what it costs to buy, sell, or transfer Bitcoins) have gone up by so much, they used to be $1 or $2 dollars and have gone up to $35 in the last 2 months. This is a major issue because people used to buy $5 items with Bitcoin, now it is only smart to buy $500 or more items. People who own Bitcoin are selling it because it is less useful, causing the price to drop. The other thing that is causing the price of Bitcoin to drop is the growth of other cryptocurrencies. The three top cryptocurrencies other than Bitcoin have been going up in price much faster than Bitcoin. Bitcoin used to be the only good cryptocurrency but cryptocurrencies like Ripple, Ethereum and Litecoin are quickly approaching Bitcoin. This means that less people are buying Bitcoin, lowering the price.

Before we learn about what caused the Litecoin crash, a quick note. These are examples of how things have crashed in the past, not necessarily how they will crash in the future. Litecoin crashed at the same time as Bitcoin, mid-December 2017. It was at $350 and then dropped to $220, which is a 37% crash. This happened for a very different reason, the volatility of cryptocurrency. Volatility means that somethings price is changing a lot each day, which normally does not happen to something with a $10 billion dollar market value. This is not true with Litecoin, because like Bitcoin, nothing is backing it, so it can change values frequently.

These are some of the ways that Bitcoin could crash in the future - other ways are also possible. For example, if Bitcoin were banned from a country, there would be a massive crash, but Bitcoin might go back up because people would buy it because the price was low.

What would happen if Bitcoin did crash? Many things that would be very bad for investors could happen, but there is also much mystery to what would happen. If there were a Bitcoin crash, a few obvious things would happen: people would lose a lot of money and a lot of Bitcoins would be sold. People would lose money with mining and with investing. When you purchase mining equipment or do cloud mining, you are paid in a fixed amount of Bitcoins. If that fixed amount of Bitcoins is not worth much, you could have spent $10,000 on mining and make $10 in Bitcoin per year. The second way that people would lose money if Bitcoin crashes is if they had bought a lot of Bitcoin. If someone had their life savings invested in Bitcoin and Bitcoin crashed, they could lose it all. Because the price dropped, investors would likely sell their Bitcoin because they do not want to lose more money. This is because of supply and demand, when the price goes down, the demand goes up, which makes the price go up because people will want to buy it at a cheap price. This creates a weird concept because, when the price goes down a lot people start to buy it again until the price gets really high, then the price goes down again. That is how it works for Bitcoin – it is a big cycle. At the time of this writing Bitcoin is at about $11,000 and in a few months from now if might crash to $10 or might skyrocket to $1 million. If it goes down to $10 the price will go up until people start to sell it and it goes back down. One last thing to say in this section, depending on how much Bitcoin crashes by, the results would be very different.

Will it crash? Nobody knows that for sure, but I do have a prediction. If Bitcoins price goes up to $50,000 in the next two or three months, it is possible that Bitcoin will crash. It is rare that an asset can gain value so quickly, which could be what causes Bitcoin to crash. A good way to think about this is the expression: "a fire that burns too bright will burn out quickly." Bitcoin has already crashed twice, and I think it is likely to happen again. In 2024 when the last Bitcoin will be mined, I predict that the price of Bitcoin will go up a lot because of the people trying to buy Bitcoin, but the miners who will want to cash out will crash Bitcoin. It is likely that

Bitcoin will also surge, and the price will skyrocket. If the price of Bitcoin stays somewhere in between $10,000-$20,000 it is unlikely that there will be crash in early 2018.

With that said, let's look at what would happen to Bitcoin's price in different scenarios. The first and most drastic scenario is if Bitcoin got banned in China. In China Bitcoin is heavily used, and if all Bitcoin holders in China had to sell their Bitcoins at once, the price could go down a lot. This would also affect other countries because it would make people fear that Bitcoin could get banned in their country. This would lead to more people selling their Bitcoin, which could crash the price by perhaps as much as 90%.

This scenario is unlikely but what more likely would cause Bitcoin to crash in the near future is if a major exchange got hacked. One more thing about crashes, they could happen at any time. Always be prepared for a crash, because if you are not, you could put in too much money and lose it all.

Congratulations on learning about Bitcoin crashing, you learned what a crash was, what could cause a crash, what would happen if Bitcoin did crash and if it will crash. The most important thing about this chapter is the fact that Bitcoin could crash at any time for any reason, and to be prepared.

Fun Fact: If you bought a Big Mac from McDonalds with Bitcoin, the transaction fees would cost as much as nine Big Macs.

Ethereum

This chapter is going to be different - instead of learning about Bitcoin, we will be learning about Ethereum. Ethereum is a type of cryptocurrency that uses blockchain but is different in many ways from Bitcoin. In this chapter, we are going to learn three things: what is Ethereum (introduction), how it is different than Bitcoin, and the purpose of Ethereum.

What is Ethereum? There are two things related to Ethereum that are different but connected, Ether and Ethereum. Ethereum is a platform (tool) that people can use to create their own cryptocurrency. Ether is a cryptocurrency that is used just like Bitcoin, but is used for the transaction costs of the cryptocurrencies people make (it is also a cryptocurrency on its own). Ethereum is great because normally you would have to write thousands of lines of code and then convert it to a cryptocurrency, but it is much easier with Ethereum. Anybody can create a cryptocurrency with it, which has led to thousands of cryptocurrencies being created with Ethereum. You can create cryptocurrency with a programming language called Solidity.

These cryptocurrencies are based off something called a smart contract (we talked about this in the blockchain chapter), which is the set of rules the cryptocurrency follows. These rules can be anything. For example, you could program it to add one to everyone's balance if it rains. The ability to make smart contracts is what makes all Ethereum-based cryptocurrencies unique. Ethereum is sometimes referred to as "programmable money." A good way to think of Ethereum versus Ether is as follows: Ethereum is a toy maker, and Ether is a toy. With Bitcoin, when you make a transaction you have to pay with Bitcoin but with Ethereum, you have to pay with Ether. The market capitalization of Ether (which is the total number of Ether times the value per Ether) is over $70 billion dollars, and has grown over 9,000% in 2017 alone. The goal of Ethereum is simple. While normally companies like Google and Apple control what you can do on an app, Ethereum wants everybody to be able to do what they want with their money. Ether is a cryptocurrency that can be used in the same ways as Bitcoin, like buying things or mining.

Ethereum was created by a man from Russia named Vitalik Buterin, who is only 23. If he only kept 1% of all Ether he would have $700 million dollars. One of the craziest things about Ether is the fact that five Ether are mined every 12-14 seconds. This means that 18 million Ether are created each year, which is why the price will probably never be as high as Bitcoin.

One more topic before we dive into the details of Ethereum. Ethereum might take over Bitcoin. Bitcoin has only one function, an online payment system, but Ethereum is that but more. With Ethereum, you can make online payments and you can create cryptocurrencies.

Now, let's compare Bitcoin to Ethereum and find out which is better, and which is more useful.

Bitcoin Vs Ethereum: Bitcoin and Ethereum have two basic similarities: they run on blockchain, and they are tradeable. Other than that, they are very different. A big difference is that Ethereum helps people create decentralized applications, and can also be used for things unrelated to cryptocurrency. One of the big advantages of Ethereum is that it is a technology that is not just used for cryptocurrency. Decentralized applications will affect everything in the future. Here is a example of what decentralized means. Imagine that there are two data servers, one stores everybody's data in a warehouse, and you have to trust that they will keep it safe. The other data server is broken up into 1,000 pieces that are stored at each person's house. The second option is decentralized because all the information is stored with everybody, not in one central place. Another big advantage that Ethereum has is that Ether and other Ethereum-based cryptocurrencies are created with smart contracts. Smart contracts are basically how Bitcoin was created, but much more complicated. Because of that, Ethereum is equal to Bitcoin in terms of the technology behind their cryptocurrency.

One of the advantages of Bitcoin is the fact that it takes ten minutes to mine 12.5 Bitcoins, while it would take 36 seconds to mine 15 Ether. This is an issue with Ether because it is so easy to mine, making it less valuable. If

Ether's price gets too high, the fact that it is easy to mine Ether could be what causes it to crash.

Deciding which of these currencies is better is not a good measure, because they have different goals. The goal of Ethereum is to allow people to use Ether, but also create their own cryptocurrencies. Bitcoin is a form of digital money that runs on blockchain.

There are, however, some big differences in between Ether and Bitcoin. Bitcoin transaction fees are around $35, while Ether transaction fees are around 60 cents. This is yet another advantage for Ether and Ethereum, because people who create cryptocurrencies do not have to pay as much Ether, and an advantage for Ether because low transaction fees make a cryptocurrency better to use. There is no right answer to which is better, it depends on what you are going to use it for.

I believe that Bitcoin is better for a long-term investment, but I think Ether is a better for low scale things like buying things online, sending Ether as a gift, and short-term investing. This is true for two reasons: the transaction costs and the fact that Bitcoin has been around for much longer than Ether. If you tried to pay for something online with Bitcoin, it would not be smart because the transaction costs could be more than the item, making Ether better for buying things like t-shirts. The second and last thing I want to talk about in this section of the Ethereum chapter, is the fact that Bitcoin is more established. If you have an issue with Ether or

Ethereum, there are not as many people who can help you as there are for Bitcoin. As Ether grows and establishes itself it will become a more widely known and used currency.

What is the point of Ethereum? Ethereum as we know is both a blockchain platform and a cryptocurrency. First, we will look at the point of Ether than the point of the Ethereum blockchain platform. Ether is very similar to Bitcoin in its use, as it can be used for online purchases, investing, and as a payment receiving method, but Ether also has one feature Bitcoin does not: it is gas. In terms of cryptocurrency, gas is what is used for transactions and how people run their cryptocurrencies. For example, if I decided I wanted to make a special cryptocurrency for someone's birthday, I would need gas to "fuel" the transaction. This is what makes Ethereum so great - Ether has the same functionality of Bitcoin but can be used in the Ethereum platform. Ether could be effective if it only had one of its two great futures. If Ether was just a cryptocurrency, nothing else, Ether would just be another Bitcoin with lower transaction costs. If Ether was just the fuel for transactions of cryptocurrencies people create, it would be the fundamental tool in a powerful technology, Ethereum.

Speaking of Ethereum, let's talk about the purpose of Ethereum and what it can do for business. To understand this we first have to know what an ICO is. ICO stands for initial coin offering, and is how new cryptocurrencies first get onto the market. Companies do this as a way of raising money, by saying things like "buy our cryptocurrency and you could be a millionaire."

So how does Ethereum have to do with ICOs? Ethereum is a massive help for people trying to do an ICO, because you can make a cryptocurrency in a few hours with Ethereum. You can also launch an ICO easily with online services. Normally the process of creating a cryptocurrency could take months or years. Ethereum at the very least is a big time saver.

Ethereum not just can be used for cryptocurrency-related things, it can be used for voting along with many other things. Blockchain itself will revolutionize technology, but now with Ethereum, blockchain-related applications are now closer to taking over many industries. Blockchain could be used to keep track of voting, keeping information protected (encryption), and many yet to be discovered revolutionary technologies. To sum it all up in six words, "Ethereum makes making blockchain applications easier."

Congratulations on finishing this chapter on Ethereum. It is good to have information on other types of cryptocurrencies. You learned what Ethereum is, what Ether is, what is the difference between Ethereum and Bitcoin, and the purpose of Ethereum. One thing to remember, "Blockchain will change everything, and Ethereum is the tool that will allow people to utilize blockchain's power."

Fun Fact: Ethereum was created by a 19 year old, Vitalik Buterin. 50 of his cryptocurrency, Ether, could pay for a full year of college. While most kids his age were still focusing on getting into college, he focused on creating a $70 billion dollar blockchain platform.

ICOs

ICOs might be the future of company funding or the next best investment. In this chapter, we are going to learn what an ICO is, if ICOs are good investments, and if they are the future of funding.

What is an ICO? An ICO is a form of fundraising where companies create and sell a cryptocurrency. ICOs are very similar to something called an IPO, initial public offering. IPOs are when a company sells their shares to investors for money. ICOs sell their cryptocurrencies for money.

These cryptocurrencies can be used kind of like a token at an arcade. Normally you can do two things with cryptocurrency from an ICO: exchange it for other cryptocurrencies, or use it within the company. When I say use it within the company, I mean that the companies who issue the ICO will have deals like "one terabyte of data storage for ten ICO coins." Major cryptocurrencies like Ethereum have done ICOs because of its power to raise money without capital. In a way, ICOs are a lot like Kickstarter but for cryptocurrency.

The best part of ICOs is the fact that anyone anywhere can launch an ICO and raise capital. To create a cryptocurrency, all you need to do is follow some online guides. One major disadvantage of ICOs is its massive potential to crash. Because so much money is being raised through ICOs every day, people are going to start to realize that these tokens are too easy to create. Anything that takes a few weeks to make and could make you millions of dollars could be seen as fraud. It is easy to scam people with ICOs because there is nothing in the real world backing it up.

That said, ICOs have been what has enabled some of the top cryptocurrencies on the market. If you invested $1 in the Ethereum ICO, you would have over $2,400 right now. ICOs can be used for fundraising cryptocurrency related and unrelated projects. The companies who launch these usually need money to build their company. In return for your investment, if the cryptocurrency does well, you could make a fortune. If you purchase ICO coins, you can store the coins you bought with an Ethereum wallet (assuming that the coins were created using Ethereum).

One last thing about ICOs before we talk about investing in ICOs is the issue that they might not be legally protected. If you get scammed and get your money stolen with an ICO, it is possible that the government cannot do anything about it. There are three things to look out for to not get scammed: guaranteed returns, too good to be true, and fake urgency. Most billionaire investors make less than 30% in a year, so making 1,000% in one day will not happen. Always be wary of anything with "massive guaranteed returns." Second, if what the ICO website says seems too good to be true, it probably is. No investment is too good to be true. Last, fraudulent ICOs will try to say things like "only one minute to buy" or "don't miss out, make $1 million in five minutes." This is their trick to make people buy without thinking. I suggest you only invest in ICOs that seem realistic.

Investing in ICOs? In some situations, people have made millions of dollars off a small investment, but in others people have lost their life savings with a bad investment. If you are going to invest in ICOs there are three things that will maximize your chance of making money.

The first is to be aware that all the hype about ICOs may die down. Right now people are making very high returns, but no investment will ever do this forever. As more people catch on to what ICOs are, they will become so common that the value will be diluted. The way people make money with ICOs is because investors, three years in the future, cannot get the currency at such a low price and are willing to pay more for it.

The second thing that will allow for you to be successful investing in ICOs is to understand what you are investing in. Think about it like this: you have to buy one of two boxes that are both the same price. Would you rather take a random guess as to which box was better, or would you rather know what was inside. One box had gold and the other box had trash - if you guessed you would have a 50% chance of getting the gold. But if you knew exactly what was inside, you would have a 100% chance of getting the gold. This is the same thing with ICOs, for example with Ethereum. They had hundreds of pages of information because they were reliable. Because anyone can make an ICO, the ICOs with a lot of information that makes sense, are the ones that will make you money because they are less likely to be a random person trying to get rich quick online.

Before we look at the third thing that can help you invest in ICOs, let's quickly revisit one concept we already talked about: guarantees. Even if you spend over 100 hours researching and believe that the ICO will be successful, it could still fail. To explain why ICOs do these things we need to make an analogy using boxes. This time there are three boxes, one with real gold, one with trash, and one with fake gold that looks just like real gold. If you guess without looking, you have a one in three chance of getting the real gold. But, if you look you will have a one in two chance, not one in one because even though you looked, you could still have picked the fake gold. This is what investors do, they look at all the ICOs, narrow it down and then guess. ICOs can be risky because they have such a high reward that the chances that it fails significantly increases.

Now for the last way to invest in ICOs: invest in cryptocurrencies you would use if you were not an investor. The only thing that would give cryptocurrency value is if people like using it. This is because the price is a balance of supply and demand. If the coin is bad, there will be no demand and the price will go down. If you think that you would not want to use the cryptocurrency the ICO is using, it is not a good investment. With that said, one thing to remember about investing in ICOs, the people who buy a good cryptocurrency first are the one who make all the money.

Are ICOs the future of fundraising? ICOs are one of the most different ways of fundraising, and there is much to learn about them. In this section of the ICOs chapter, we are going to learn about fundraising with ICOs.

Before we go into detail, let's take a look at one of the huge advantages of raising money with an ICO: speed. Unlike traditional ways of raising money, where it could take months or years, ICOs can raise millions in hours. This, however, is not always the case, but if you are a company and can raise millions in less than a day, it is a very good option. ICOs, like Kickstarter, allow anyone to launch an ICO and raise money. This means that for small companies as well as big companies, fundraising with an ICO is possible. The fees to launch an ICO, if you are using a popular launching service, could be less than a few hundred dollars.

Now let's look at some downsides of fundraising with ICOs, before we decide if ICOs are the future of fundraising. Because there are so many ICOs for people to invest in, to have a good ICO, it might take a lot of time and resources to make a good product. The biggest downside to fundraising with ICOs is the fact that ICOs are a luck game. When those companies raise $20 million, it is not that they are so much better, it is because they got lucky. This is not true for all ICOs. Ethereum went on to become one of the biggest cryptocurrencies in the world. When they launched their ICO, they had a cryptocurrency that was worth buying so they made millions in a few days.

Now that we looked at some pros and cons, let's now decide if in fact ICOs are a good way of fundraising. There are three things that make ICOs good fundraising methods: speed, security, and cost. In the future as well as right now, the quicker you get startup capital (money), the quicker you can start your company. For companies who need money fast, ICOs will be what allows them to make it.

In a few years applications using blockchain will be much more common, which means that more and more people will use ICOs to raise money. ICOs are the only good way that a blockchain/cryptocurrency based application can raise money. IPOs are very hard and expensive to launch, because making it secure is hard. With blockchain, people launching ICOs will be able to have that level security for very cheap. Launching an ICO might only cost a few hundred dollars, which is why small companies will use it to fundraise. Imagine you are someone with a great idea but needs funding, and you only have $100. You only have two options: Kickstarter and ICOs. ICOs are a better option because cryptocurrency can increase in value if your company is good.

Lastly, let's talk about returns, because it is possible that you could make millions of dollars with an ICO, the return on investment could end up being much more than huge. For example, if you start an ICO and keep 10% of your cryptocurrency, and it becomes worth 1 cent, you could make $1,000,000 if you established 1 billion cryptocurrency coins.

To finish up this chapter, I would like to say one more thing: "the quickest way to make $1 million in a day is to get people to invest in your ICO, and have a coin that people want to use."

Congratulations on finishing this chapter on ICOs you learned what they were and how they work, how to invest and why to invest, and why ICOs are the future of fundraising. Remember, ICOs may be a quick way to make money, but you could also get scammed.

Fun Fact: If you invested $320 in the Ethereum ICO, you would have approximately $1 million dollars right now in January 2018.

Appendix A: Useful Resources

I made a list of the best resources to learn about Bitcoin other than this book. If you read/watch the information on these ten resources, you can learn a lot about Bitcoin and build on your knowledge from this book.

1: https://blockgeeks.com
2: youtube.com
3: https://Bitcoin.org/en/
4: https://en.Bitcoin.it/wiki/Main_Page
5:https://www.khanacademy.org/economics-finance-domain/core-finance/money-and-banking/Bitcoin/v/Bitcoin-what-is-it
6: https://www.investopedia.com/terms/b/Bitcoin.asp
7: https://www.coindesk.com/information/
8: https://bitconnect.co/Bitcoin-information
9: https://academy.Bitcoin.com/#/welcome
10: https://www.digitaltrends.com/computing/how-to-buy-Bitcoins/

Appendix B: 12 Cool Bitcoin Products/Services

Here are some cool Bitcoin products and services that I recommend using/buying.

1. Coinbase is an exchange where you can buy Bitcoin, Bitcoin cash, Ether, and Litecoin. They charge very low fees and you can get your cryptocurrency instantly. Also, they have two-step verification to store your cryptocurrency securely. https://www.coinbase.com/join/5a3547a783640c0705 bbe8df

2. Hashflare is a cloud mining service, you can buy hash rate cheap and earn Bitcoin every day. You can reinvest the Bitcoins you earn every day for compound interest. Hashflare is a good way to make an extra income every day.

3. I Accept Bitcoin T-Shirt

4. Bitcoin Collector's Set - Limited Edition

5. Bitcoin Gold Necklace Shirt

6. Gray Crew Bitcoin Dress Socks

7. Leather Bitcoin Watch

8. 5 Panel Flat 2 Tone Mesh Bitcoin Hat

9. Gold Plated Bitcoin Keychain BitcoinBling

10. Silk Bitcoin Neck Tie

11. Oval Bitcoin Logo Bumper Sticker

12. 11 Oz Bitcoin Coffee Mug

Appendix C: Sources

Thank you to all the sources of information that I used to do research for this book.

https://www.lifewire.com/what-are-Bitcoins-2483146
https://www.khanacademy.org/computing/computer-science/cryptography/crypt/v/intro-to-cryptography
https://digiconomist.net/Bitcoin-energy-consumption
https://www.statista.com/statistics/247280/number-of-Bitcoins-in-circulation/
https://www.lifewire.com/cryptocoin-mining-for-beginners-2483064
https://www.investopedia.com/tech/how-does-Bitcoin-mining-work/
https://arstechnica.com/tech-policy/2017/12/how-Bitcoin-works/
https://www.howtogeek.com/141374/htg-explains-what-is-Bitcoin-and-how-does-it-work/
http://www.businessinsider.com/Bitcoin-history-cryptocurrency-satoshi-nakamoto-2017-12/#two-years-later-the-mysterious-figure-known-as-satoshi-nakamoto-disappears-from-the-web-6
https://futurism.com/images/the-entire-history-of-Bitcoin-in-a-single-infographic/
https://en.Bitcoin.it/wiki
http://www.businessinsider.com/Bitcoin-pizza-10000-100-million-2017-11
https://www.theverge.com/2014/2/26/5450206/who-stole-400-million-from-mt-gox

https://blockgeeks.com/guides/what-is-blockchain-technology/

https://medium.com/@micheledaliessi/how-does-the-blockchain-work-98c8cd01d2ae

http://www.businessinsider.com/what-is-blockchain-2016-3/#blockchains-are-ledgers-like-excel-spreadsheets-but-they-accept-inputs-from-lots-of-different-parties-the-ledger-can-only-be-changed-when-there-is-a-consensus-among-the-group-that-makes-them-more-secure-and-it-means-theres-no-need-for-a-central-authority-to-approve-transactions-1

IBM blockchain for dummies book

https://blockgeeks.com/guides/smart-contracts/#

https://www.Ethereum.org/

https://solidity.readthedocs.io/en/develop/introduction-to-smart-contracts.html

https://Ethereumbuilders.gitbooks.io/guide/content/en/solidity_tutorials.html

http://www.theasianbanker.com/updates-and-articles/initial-coin-offerings-from-bubble-to-the-future-of-fundraising

https://www.shapingtomorrow.com/home/alert/665529-Future-of--Blockchain

https://www.accenture.com/us-en/insight-blockchain-technology-how-banks-building-real-time

https://www.investopedia.com/news/could-cryptocurrencies-replace-cash-Bitcoin-flippening/

https://steemit.com/cryptocurrency/@devildat/will-Bitcoin-soon-replace-paper-money

https://coinmarketcap.com/all/views/all/

https://www.investopedia.com/terms/b/Bitcoin-wallet.asp

https://99Bitcoins.com/what-is-Bitcoin-wallet-bwbt-3/
http://coinoutletatm.com/7-types-of-Bitcoin-wallets/
https://www.youtube.com/watch?time_continue=7&v=Y4
0Cn13Y5Ng
https://www.Bitcoinmining.com/
https://Bitcoin.stackexchange.com/questions/8031/what-are-Bitcoin-miners-really-solving
https://www.cryptocompare.com/mining/calculator/btc?HashingPower=4.73&HashingUnit=TH%2Fs&PowerConsumption=.25&CostPerkWh=
 http://bigthink.com/strange-maps/Bitcoin-consumes-more-energy-than-159-individual-countries
https://www.coinwarz.com/calculators/Bitcoin-mining-calculator/?h=459.00&p=0.00&pc=0.10&pf=0.00&d=1873105475221.61000000&r=12.50000000&er=4500&hc=0.00
https://arstechnica.com/tech-policy/2017/12/a-brief-history-of-Bitcoin-hacks-and-frauds/
https://www.theguardian.com/technology/2014/mar/18/history-of-Bitcoin-hacks-alternative-currency
https://coinsutra.com/biggest-Bitcoin-hacks/
https://Bitcoinmagazine.com/articles/bitfloor-hacked-250000-missing-1346821046/
https://en.wikipedia.org/wiki/Bitfinex_hack
https://www.coindesk.com/bitfinex-Bitcoin-hack-know-dont-know/
http://www.altcointoday.com/how-bitfinex-was-hacked/
https://www.imore.com/how-touch-id-works
https://www.investopedia.com/articles/investing/082914/basics-buying-and-investing-Bitcoin.asp

https://www.fool.com/investing/2017/08/11/so-you-want-to-invest-in-Bitcoin-heres-what-you-sh.aspx

https://Bitcoinfees.info/

http://www.businessinsider.com/Bitcoin-payment-mining-fees-hit-new-high-2017-12

http://www.businessinsider.com/Bitcoin-Bitcoin-cash-Ethereum-Litecoin-crash-on-friday-december-22-2017-12

https://www.cnbc.com/2017/12/26/Bitcoin-price-in-2018-could-hit-60000-but-another-crash-is-coming.html

https://www.fastfoodmenuprices.com/mcdonalds-prices/?redir

https://blockgeeks.com/guides/Ethereum/

https://www.investopedia.com/articles/investing/031416/Bitcoin-vs-Ethereum-driven-different-purposes.asp

https://www.coindesk.com/information/Ethereum-mining-works/

https://www.digitaltrends.com/computing/Ethereum-vs-Bitcoin/

https://bitinfocharts.com/comparison/Ethereum-transactionfees.html

http://coinnoob.com/Ethereum-real-world-use

https://www.youtube.com/watch?v=fwqa_XYzxdg

https://www.youtube.com/watch?v=iyuZ_bCQeIE

http://cryptorials.io/beginners-guide-ico-crowdsales/

https://www.sec.gov/oiea/investor-alerts-and-bulletins/ib_coinofferings

https://bitinfocharts.com/comparison/Ethereum-transactionfees.html

https://en.bitcoin.it/wiki/Private_key

https://www.thebalance.com/bitcoin-glossary-391211

https://learncryptography.com/hash-functions/what-are-hash-functions

https://bitcoin.org/en/vocabulary#signature

https://commons.wikimedia.org/wiki/File:TUX_G2.svg

Appendix D: 25 Cryptocurrency Vocabulary Words

Altcoin - A cryptocurrency based on blockchain that is not Bitcoin.

Bit - A millionth of a Bitcoin.

Bitcoin - A cryptocurrency based on blockchain created in 2009.

Bitcoin Wallet - The software that holds your copy of the ledger and your Bitcoin.

Block - The group of transactions that is mined every ten minutes and contains 12.5 Bitcoins.

Blockchain - A technology that allows for copies of a ledger to be distributed among cryptocurrency users and updates the ledger when transactions are made.

Cloud Mining - Purchasing mining equipment that is maintained and stored in someone else's facility and receiving the Bitcoins it mines. The mining equipment you buy is put in the provider's pool and you get the Bitcoin from the pool.

Crash - When the value of something drops by 25% or more.

Cold Storage - Storing Bitcoin on something not connected to the internet.

Cryptocurrency - A digitally traded currency that runs on blockchain.

Decentralized - When all of the data is stored in many places not centralized in one place.

Gas - What is used to pay the transaction fee.

Hashing - To take a word or piece of data and convert it into a hexadecimal number.

Hash Rate - A unit of processing power that represents how fast a computer can do something.

Hexadecimal Number - A number that can be made of the following digits: 0, 1, 2, 3, 4, 5, 6, 7, 8, 9, A, B, C, D, E, F.

Hot Wallet - A Bitcoin wallet that is on a internet-connected piece of hardware.

ICO - Initial Coin Offering: a sale of a cryptocurrency before it is launched to exchanges.

Ledger - The list of all Bitcoin transactions in history that is distributed to all Bitcoin users.

Mining - The process when miners verify transactions to earn Bitcoin.

Pool Mining - A group of miners that mine Bitcoin with all their miners and distribute the Bitcoin based on how much processing power each person contributes.

Private Key - The 256-bit number that is used to keep your account secure.

Public Key - Your wallet address that consists of numbers and letters.

Smart Contract - A piece of software that controls the actions of a cryptocurrency.

Transaction Fee - The cost of buying or selling a cryptocurrency.

Volatile Cryptocurrency - A cryptocurrency that changes value significantly on a daily basis.

About Me

My name is Andrew Courey and I am a middle school student. I live in Massachusetts and do all of my writing in my office (i.e. the cove in my room with a desk). I play basketball and have an interest in business, and I hope to start a company. I watch Shark Tank regularly, and perhaps will have a chance to present a business plan, though I do not want to give up any equity. Also, I have been reading The Everything Store about Jeff Bezos – that is how I found out about Kindle Direct Publishing.

Here is my story on how I wrote this book. In late November, while I was researching investments, I stumbled across something called Bitcoin. Every day I would spend hours researching Bitcoin, by reading articles, books, asking my Uncle, and watching hours of YouTube. It was then when I knew that I wanted to share this knowledge with other people. My Dad suggested I write a book, I said ok and started writing. I wrote every day after school and all day over school break. Finally, I had one chapter to go and I felt like I could not keep writing and wanted to take a break. I woke up early the next day and said to myself "I will finish this chapter today," and finished four hours after that. Over the next few days, I edited and added new things in, and eventually I was finished. I had written my first book!

Then, of course, my parents taught me the hard part - editing. I was so excited to publish it immediately, but worked for weeks on editing until I knew it was ready. I published it on Kindle, and then ordered paper copies to give to my teachers.

Here I am now, with you reading my book about Bitcoin. It has been a great journey creating this book, and I hope you enjoyed it.

Thank you for reading. If you have any questions, email me at andrewcourey34goldenmamba@gmail.com.

Best regards,

Andrew K. Courey

Printed in Great Britain
by Amazon